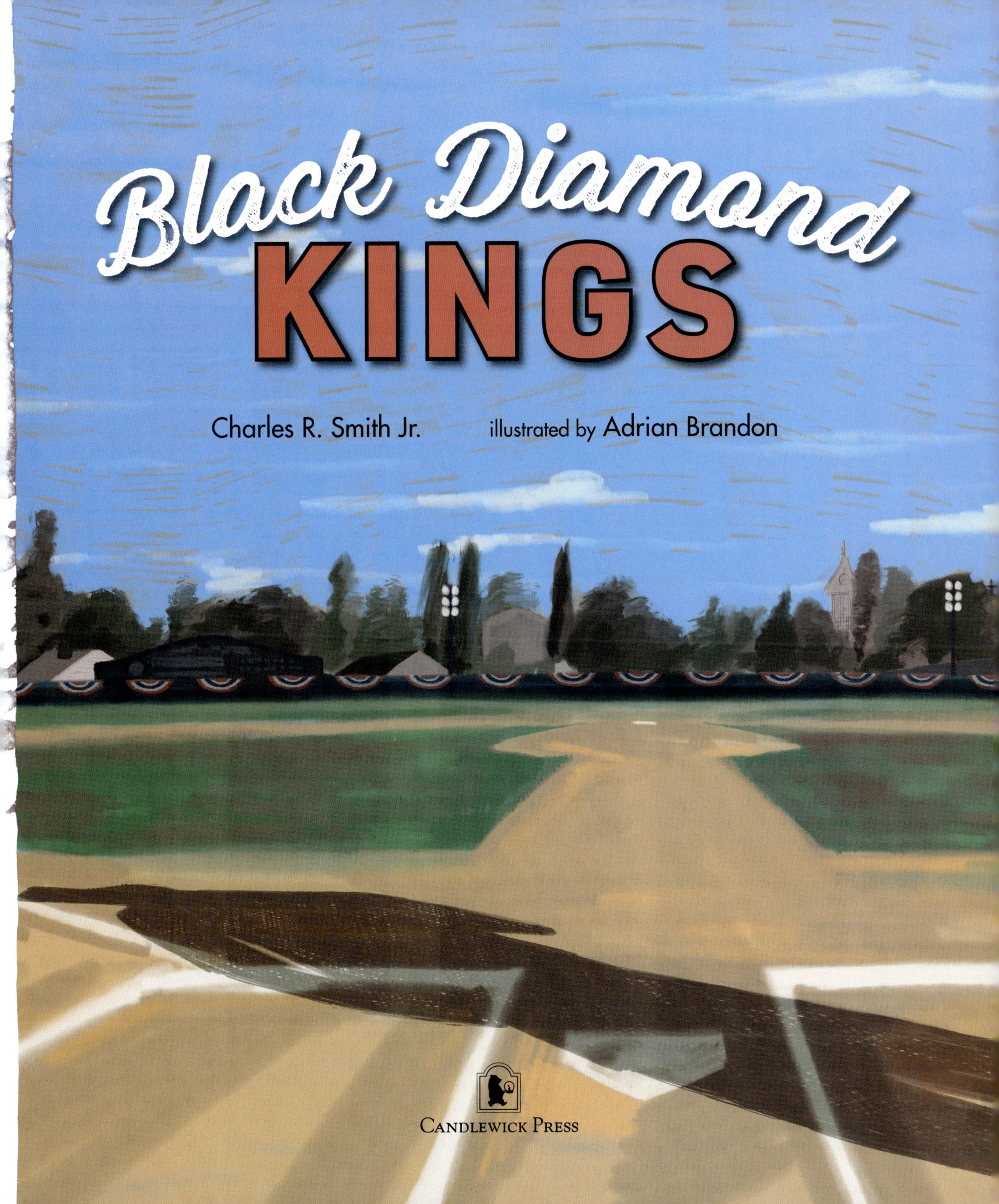

Black Diamond KINGS

Charles R. Smith Jr.   illustrated by Adrian Brandon

CANDLEWICK PRESS

INTRODUCING

Leroy Robert "Satchel" Paige

Ladies and gentlemen,
the man you came to see,
strolling onto the field
cool
and confidently,
a tall drink of water
with long legs
and a strong arm,
the hurler of pitches
like Trouble Ball
and Long Tom,
the Bat Dodger,
Bee Ball,
Wobbly Ball
and Hesitation Pitch,
the magician on the mound
with the endless bag of tricks
with his windmill windup
and high-leg kick,
makes batters disappear
with a quick flick of the wrist.

Fans, there he stands
the Picasso on the hill
ready to paint strikes
with finesse and skill.
So get out of your seat
for the hurler of heat,
the maestro of movement,
the legend you came to see,
some say the greatest
pitcher in history.
The man
the myth
standing tall
center stage,
ladies and gentlemen,
the great
Satchel Paige!

THUNDER AND LIGHTNING

Josh Gibson

Here comes big Josh
big Josh
up to bat,
here comes big Josh
with the thunder in his bat.

Here comes the heat
speeding fast
fast
fast,
here it comes
there it goes
with a thunderous
CRASH.

There it goes
there it goes
OUT
of the stadium,
a bolt of lightning from the bat of big Josh Gibson!

SMOOTH

Walter Fenner "Buck" Leonard

Smooth
with the swing
like
a hot knife
through butter.

Smooth
with the glove
like
stones skipping
across water.

Smooth
with the arm
like
a slingshot
so strong.

Smooth
with a cool head
like
the calm
in a storm.

Smooth with the bat
smooth with the glove
smooth captain Buck,
the man teammates and fans love!

POP
John Henry "Pop" Lloyd

Pop at the plate
Pop on the hill
Pop on base
Pop in the field.
Pop with the scoop
Pop with the stop
Pop with the swing
Pop with the pop!

DANCING AT THE HOT CORNER

Ray Dandridge

Hooks on the hot corner
moving like a cat,
pouncing and leaping
at the crack
of the bat.

Hooks on the hot corner
dancing with the slide
with the pick
with the pluck
with the spin
with the dive.

Hooks on the hot corner
dancing off the bag,
hard charging bunts
making bare-handed grabs.

Hooks on the hot corner
with the smooth throw
from his back
from his knees
or pirouetting on his toes.

Hooks on the hot corner
bow-legged and squat,
hooking everything
at the hot corner spot!

A SONNET FOR SHAKESPEARE

Willie Wells

Shall I compare thee to a summer's day?
Watching Willie Wells perform at shortstop
brings joy to the heart with each finished play,
brings a smile with each first base glove pop.
Our eyes see Willie focused intensely,
reading the batter preparing to swing,
ready to range with no hesitancy,
reacting when the crack of the bat rings.
Swift-moving feet track down balls hit with might,
sliding and scooping and spinning to throw,
flashing the leather like bright summer light;
shining on the diamond, Willie's glove glows.
     So long as hands can clap and eyes can see,
     Willie, the Shakespeare of shortstops, is thee.

FAST AS WHAT?

James "Cool Papa" Bell

"Cool Papa was so fast, he could turn the lights off and be under the covers before the room was dark."

"Cool Papa was so fast, he once hit a line drive up the middle and was hit by the ball sliding into second!"

"Cool Papa was so fast, he scored from first off a sacrifice bunt."

"Cool Papa was so fast, he hit an inside-the-park home run and circled the bases in thirteen seconds."

"I heard twelve."

"Cool Papa was so fast that one time he bunted a ball down the third base line and the pitcher tagged him out sliding into third."

"Cool Papa was so fast, he could steal two bases on one pitch."

"Cool Papa was so fast that when Jesse Owens raced players before the start of Negro League games, he refused to race Cool Papa."

"Cool Papa was so fast that when he hit a dribbler back to the pitcher, the infielders would yell 'Hurry!'"

"How fast was Cool Papa?"
        Finger snap.
        "Faster than that."

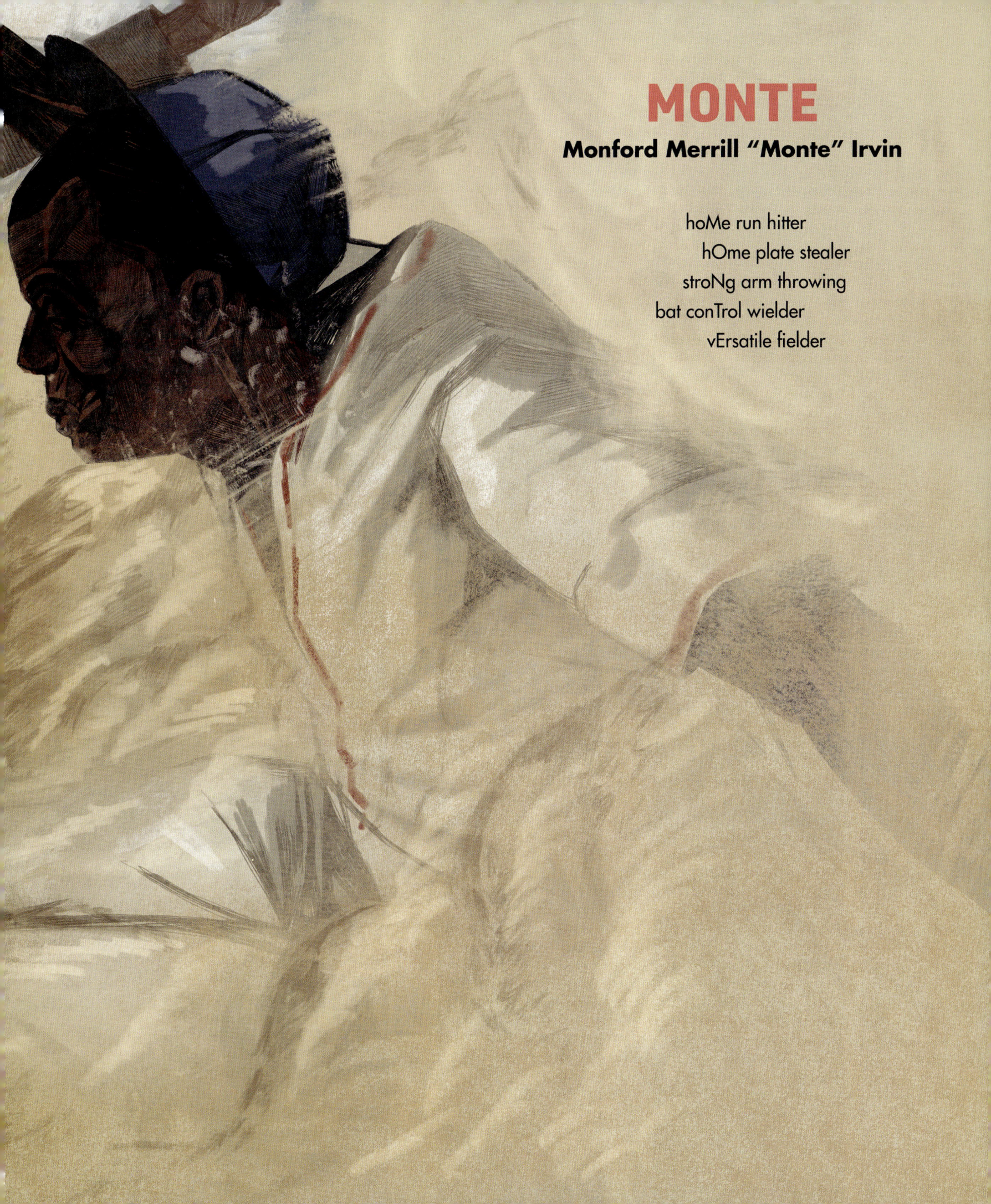

MONTE

Monford Merrill "Monte" Irvin

hoMe run hitter
hOme plate stealer
stroNg arm throwing
bat conTrol wielder
vErsatile fielder

FIVE-TOOL TURKEY

Norman "Turkey" Stearnes

Swat, Turkey, swat
make it
fly, Turkey, fly
send another ball soaring
up high through the sky.

Hit, Turkey, hit
run, Turkey, run
first base
second base
third base
done.

Dig, Turkey, dig
steal, Turkey, steal
slide in
stand up
no big deal.

Go, Turkey, go
chase, Turkey, chase
catch it, Turkey
catch it
keep the runner
on the base.

Trot, Turkey, trot
now
throw, Turkey, throw
throw it home
from outfield,
go, Turkey, go.

That's our Turkey
out there playing ball,
our five-tool Turkey
'cause he can do it all!

O-S-C-A-R

Oscar Charleston

Orchestrator outwits outmatched opponents.
Sharp-eyed southpaw slashes singles, smacks skyscrapers.
Consistently clutch, center-field cheetah captivates crowds.
Aggressive attitude attracts attacks.
Remarkable recruiter recommended Robinson.

SMOKE
"Smokey" Joe Williams

Standing tall
on the hill
eyes focused
under his bill,
twirling
the ball,
waiting
to thrill
fans in the stands
and
teammates on the field,
the feared flamethrower
Smokey Joe Will,
known to burn bats
with precision and skill.
The match gets lit
with a long-leg kick
and the fireball flames
with an arm whip
scorching seams
spinning
sizzling
strike after strike
inning after inning
swing after swing
burning bat after bat,
torching tempers
with each batter sat,
singeing the scoreboard
to the end of the game,
Smokey Joe smokin'
living up to his name!

KICK, MULE, KICK

George "Mule" Suttles

Kick, Mule, kick!
Let's see you swing the stick,
let's see you send the ball a mile
with a mighty lick.

Kick, Mule, kick!
Get a single
get a double
get a triple
get a homer
get our team out of trouble.

Kick, Mule, kick!
Launch the low ball high,
high above the fence
out of the park into the sky.

Kick, Mule, kick!
Whatcha say
whatcha say?
Give the fans a grand story
to tell our grandkids someday.

★ PLAYER NOTES ★

LEROY ROBERT "SATCHEL" PAIGE

In any conversation about Negro league baseball, it won't take long before you hear the name Satchel Paige. Known for his speed, command, and arsenal of pitches (some of which are mentioned in his poem), Satchel Paige was also a great showman. He would sometimes show up late for games to make a grand entrance, to spectators' delight. With a long career in the Negro leagues, Paige would go on to finish in Major League Baseball, playing for the Cleveland Indians, St. Louis Browns, and Kansas City A's. Though well past his prime at that point, Paige still had enough gas in his arm and cleverness in his head to help the Cleveland Indians to the playoffs in 1948 at the age of forty-two. He kept playing until 1965, when he finally retired at the age of fifty-nine!

Years played: 1926–1950 in the Negro leagues; 1948–1953 and 1965 in Major League Baseball
Bats: Right   Throws: Right   Position: P

JOSH GIBSON

Josh Gibson was known to Negro league fans as the Black Babe Ruth. A big, strong man, he swung a big bat and was said to hit balls out of stadiums. But Gibson wasn't known just for his towering home runs. He could also hit for average and was a great catcher with a cannon in his arm. Unfortunately, Gibson never made it onto a Major League Baseball team, but fellow Negro leaguers and pro white players who competed against him in exhibitions called him the greatest hitter they ever saw. Period.

Years played: 1930–1946   Bats: Right   Throws: Right   Positions: C, OF, 3B, 1B

WALTER FENNER "BUCK" LEONARD

With a smooth swing, Buck Leonard was known to smash balls into walls and over them. Batting behind Josh Gibson, he was the left-handed half of the Thunder Twins, a powerful tandem. Their big bats anchored the Homestead Grays through nine championship seasons, ending with back-to-back titles. Sure-handed and strong at first base, Leonard was known for making plays that most white Major League Baseball players couldn't even make—and making them look easy. His dependability and cool head made him well liked and respected, not just on the Grays but throughout the Negro leagues.

Years played: 1933–1950   Bats: Left   Throws: Left   Positions: 1B, OF

JOHN HENRY "POP" LLOYD

John Henry "Pop" Lloyd was considered by many to be the best shortstop to ever play in the Negro leagues. He scooped up everything that was hit his way, including a gloveful of dirt when he fielded the ball. This earned him the nickname El Cuchara, which is Spanish for spoon or scoop. At the plate, he had pop in his bat, driving in runs and hitting the ball all over the field in the cleanup spot (the fourth hitter). Lloyd played multiple positions including pitcher before settling in as a shortstop. The nickname Pop actually came from his actions off the field: he offered guidance to young players as a father figure and always conducted himself as a gentleman.

Years played: 1906–1932   *Bats: Left*   *Throws: Right*   *Positions: SS, 2B, 1B, C, Manager*

RAY DANDRIDGE

Ray Dandridge was hailed as the best to ever play third base, also called "the hot corner" since balls are often hit there hard and fast. He had catlike reflexes and great hands, which earned him the nickname Hooks, as in "He gets his hooks on everything." And once he got his hooks on the ball, he knew what to do with it. Every play had a smooth touch, and his arm was strong and accurate. But he was also a wizard at handling the bunt up the line, charging hard to make a bare-handed grab. Small at five feet seven, Dandridge was also a solid hitter and could spray the ball all over the field.

Years played: 1933–1949   *Bats: Right*   *Throws: Right*   *Positions: 3B, 2B, SF, OF*

WILLIE WELLS

Willie Wells was considered the best shortstop in Black baseball from the 1930s to the early 1940s. His ability to read hitters and know where to position himself gave him a jump on the ball. He used that jump to make up for a weak yet accurate arm with a quick release. Using a glove with a hole in the middle, he used sure hands to make difficult plays look easy. This earned him the nickname the Shakespeare of Shortstops, since he put on a show. I took inspiration for his poem from one of Shakespeare's most well-known sonnets. A sonnet is a structured poem that Shakespeare made famous, writing 154 of them!

Years played: 1924–1948   *Bats: Right*   *Throws: Right*   *Positions: SS, 3B, 2B, P, Manager*

JAMES "COOL PAPA" BELL

Perhaps no one in the Negro leagues has more "Is that true?" stories than James "Cool Papa" Bell. Bell had a reputation as the fastest man in the game, and he used his speed to steal bases and field fly balls. He also had great control of his bat and could smash hits to center field or turn a well-placed bunt into a triple. Since the stories about Bell are so mythical and funny, I based his poem on some of the tall tales that Negro league and white Major League Baseball players made about his speed. Some of the tales are true, some maybe not. But the legend of Cool Papa Bell is one of the best in baseball, Black or white.

Years played: 1922–1946   Bats: Both   Throws: Left   Positions: CF, LF, 1B

MONFORD MERRILL "MONTE" IRVIN

Monte Irvin could do it all on the field. He hit for high average, slammed home runs, stole bases, had a strong arm that he used in the outfield, and played multiple positions before settling in as an outfielder. Long before Jackie Robinson broke the color line, Monte was considered the best prospect to do so. Like Jackie, he went to college, served in the military, and had the temperament, education, and skill to move to Major League Baseball. He didn't end up being the first, but he wasn't far behind, and he helped lead the New York Giants to the World Series versus the New York Yankees in 1951. The Giants would go on to lose that series, but in 1954, Monte helped the team win the World Series over the heavily favored Cleveland Indians.

Years played: 1937–1948 in the Negro leagues; 1949–1956 in Major League Baseball
Bats: Right   Throws: Right   Positions: CF, LF, SS, 3B, 1B

NORMAN "TURKEY" STEARNES

Norman Stearnes earned the nickname Turkey for how he ran on the baseball field: elbows out and arms flapping. But although he was awkward, he was fast. And he used that speed to make himself a complete player. He chased down fly balls with ease in the outfield. At the plate, if he wasn't hitting a home run, he was legging out a hard-hit double into a triple. And once he got on base, he was known to be aggressive and steal, leading the Negro leagues in stolen bases and triples at least once each in his career.

Years played: 1923–1942   Bats: Left   Throws: Left   Positions: CF, LF, 1B

OSCAR CHARLESTON

Oscar Charleston played the game with skill, smarts, and aggression. He was a strong left-handed hitter who smashed the ball all over the field and into the stands, especially in the clutch. He used his blazing speed to play a shallow center field, where he would sprint back on balls before chasing them down, to the crowd's delight. Charleston's aggressive spirit got him into scuffles on the field and off. He protected younger players, and his intelligence about the game made him a successful player-manager years before he would become a full-time manager. Oscar had an eye for talent and put it to use as a scout for the Brooklyn Dodgers. He recommended Jackie Robinson and others to the Dodgers to break the long-standing color line.

Years played: 1915–1941   Managed: 1942–1954   Bats: Left   Throws: Left
Positions: CF, 1B, Manager

"SMOKEY" JOE WILLIAMS

Many say that Satchel Paige was the best Negro league pitcher in history. But just as many, particularly those who know, will tell you that "Smokey" Joe Williams was even better. Nicknamed Smokey and Cyclone because of his fastball, Williams also had pinpoint control. He could throw the ball where he wanted and as hard as he wanted, which was plenty. He threw hard enough that twenty-strikeout games were typical and he once sat down twenty-seven batters in a twelve-inning one-hitter. When he played exhibitions against white major leaguers, Williams more than held his own, shutting down the world champ New York Giants 6–0, among other impressive performances.

Years played: 1905–1932   Bats: Right   Throws: Right   Position: P

GEORGE "MULE" SUTTLES

When George "Mule" Suttles stepped up to bat, the fans would chant, "Kick, Mule, kick," because the ball jumped off his bat as if it had been kicked by a mule. Suttles was known for his tape-measure home runs and starred in legendary stories—such as the time he hit three home runs in one inning and when he came up to bat again, the other team walked off the field. But what really made Suttles dangerous was that he could also hit for average and was known for hitting doubles and triples as much as home runs. Suttles was sturdy and reliable, playing for twenty-one years.

Years played: 1923–1944   Bats: Right   Throws: Right   Positions: 1B, RF, Manager; he also worked as an umpire

★ MORE ABOUT THE NEGRO LEAGUES ★

What were the Negro leagues?

The owners in Major League Baseball had an unofficial agreement that they would not hire Black players. This separation created baseball's color line. So the Negro leagues were born and became the professional baseball leagues for Black players.

Why were they called the Negro leagues?

During the time of segregation, Black people were referred to as *colored* or *Negro*. The term *Negro* was the most progressive at the time, so that was the name used.

Was there just one league?

There were multiple independent leagues until 1920, when the Negro National League came into existence. Years later, the Eastern Colored League and the Negro American League would join them, with the Negro American League lasting the longest, until 1962.

Were there other leagues where the players could play?

Indeed there were! Many of the players spent their winters playing in Mexico or Puerto Rico.

Did the players get paid?

The players all earned some type of pay, and as in Major League Baseball, bigger-name players earned bigger pay. And some of the players with the biggest names, such as Satchel Paige, were able to get food, lodging, and other expenses covered. The players loved playing in Mexico because they were paid well, with all expenses covered, and compared to their treatment in the United States, they were not treated differently because of their skin color.

Were the players just as good as the pros in Major League Baseball?

Some would say they were better! Whenever Negro leaguers faced Major League Baseball players in exhibitions, they held their own and often defeated the white teams. They had the respect of the white major leaguers since they proved their equal on the field of play.

Where did they play?

Many of the Major League Baseball owners rented their stadiums for use when their own teams played away games. Negro league players filled the stadiums with fans just as their white counterparts did by playing entertaining, competitive baseball.

Did the Negro leagues become part of Major League Baseball after the color line was broken?

No. In fact, as more Black players joined Major League Baseball, talent was drained from the Negro leagues, which led to smaller crowds and the leagues eventually dissolving.

How were the players recruited?

Basically through word of mouth. Managers were always on the lookout at small ball fields where former and current league players had played. And since they played games all over, they were able to scout all over.

Who attended the games?

Since the games were exciting and fun, they drew a wide audience of Black and white fans alike.

Are any Negro league players in the Baseball Hall of Fame?

Every player in this book is in the Baseball Hall of Fame in Cooperstown, New York. There are twenty-five additional players for a total of thirty-seven, proving they were worthy of competing on the same field as any other players.

And as of 2024 . . .

Negro league players have been added to Major League Baseball statistics. This changes the record books because legendary players like Babe Ruth, Ted Williams, and Ty Cobb had long-standing records replaced by Josh Gibson. Other hard hitters like Mule Suttles, Turkey Stearnes, Oscar Charleston, and Buck Leonard also made numerous lists regarding stats for the best hitters. And the Negro leagues' best pitcher, Satchel Paige, took over the third spot for all-time lowest ERA (Earned Run Average, or how many hits a pitcher gives up). And once the color line was broken, players that played in both leagues, like Jackie Robinson, got a boost in their stats as well. This change is long overdue and allows Negro league players to officially be recognized as some of the best to ever play the game.

Dedicated to my grandfather Lester Smith, who introduced the
wonderful world of Negro league baseball to me, and to all the players who
showed that skill and dedication have no color
CRS

To Nolan, Easton, Georgia, Desmond, and Emerson—you're on deck!
May your play and passion meet courage and conviction.
Uncle A loves you.
AB

First edition 2025

Library of Congress Catalog Card Number pending
ISBN 978-1-5362-2535-8

25 26 27 28 29 30 APS 10 9 8 7 6 5 4 3 2

Printed in Humen, Dongguan, China

This book was typeset in Futura.
The illustrations were sketched by hand and digitally painted.

Candlewick Press
99 Dover Street
Somerville, Massachusetts 02144

www.candlewick.com

EU Authorized Representative: HackettFlynn Ltd., 36 Cloch Choirneal,
Balrothery, Co. Dublin, K32 C942, Ireland. EU@walkerpublishinggroup.com